DATE DUE			
FE 23 '88	SE 14 '90	FEB 17 '98	
AP 21 '88	JA 2 '91	AG 10 '99	
AP 28 '88	JY 7 '92	JE 09 '01	
JA 5 '89	OC 3 '92	JE 25 '01	
MR 17 '89	OC 10 '92		
AP 18 '89	DE 2 '92	AR 19	
JY 27 '89	MR 31 '93	DE 13	
NO 24 '89	OC 7 '93		
MR 19 '90	AUG 1 '9		
MR 27 '9	AG 31 '94		
JY 7 '9	AR 06 '96		
JY 26 '90	AG 06 '97		

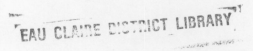

BASIC
SELF-DEFENSE
MANUAL

Fred Neff's Self-Defense Library

BASIC
SELF-DEFENSE
MANUAL

Fred Neff

Photographs by James E. Reid

Lerner Publications Company
Minneapolis

The models photographed in this book are Mike Podolinsky, Laura Phillips, Bill Polta, Rick Rowell, and Jack Engelhart.

LIBRARY OF CONGRESS CATALOGING IN PUBLICATION DATA

Neff, Fred.
   Basic self-defense manual.

   (Fred Neff's Self-Defense Library)
   Includes index.
   SUMMARY: Introduces basic principles of self-defense from the Asian fighting arts including basic exercises, stances, blocks, and escapes.

   1. Self-defense. [1. Self-defense] I. Reid, James E. II. Title. III. Title: Self-defense manual.

GV1111.N43 1976   796.8'153   75-38473
ISBN 0-8225-1152-5

Manufactured in the United States of America

International Standard Book Number: 0-8225-1152-5
Library of Congress Catalog Card Number: 75-38473

5 6 7 8 9 10 90 89 88 87 86

CONTENTS

To Mollie Neff, a unique person because of her love of beauty, her optimism, and her zest for living

PREFACE

When I became a student of karate in the 1950's, few Americans had knowledge of the Oriental fighting arts or were interested in learning them. Since that time, however, public interest in the subject has grown considerably. Today, thousands of people all over the country are studying the various fighting arts and are learning that they offer many physical, psychological, and social benefits.

This new interest and involvement in the Oriental fighting arts has created a need for books that can be used as instructional guides for beginning students. FRED NEFF'S SELF-DEFENSE LIBRARY was written to help meet that need. My purpose in writing the series was to provide a basic comprehensive course on self-defense, based on the major Oriental disciplines of karate, judo, and jujitsu. In preparing each book, I was careful to include not only the physical techniques of Oriental fighting but also the underlying philosophical principles. This is important because an understanding of both elements is required of every martial arts student. Finally, in selecting the particular self-defense techniques for each book, I tried to include techniques that could be of practical use to the average person and that could be performed effectively and safely through practice. I genuinely hope that each and every reader of the SELF-DEFENSE LIBRARY benefits as much as I have from studying the martial arts.

I would like to express my thanks and appreciation to Mr. Harry Lerner, president of Lerner Publications Company, for his enthusiasm and support in the development of this series. I would also like to thank my students, who contributed their time and skill to demonstrating the various fighting techniques in the books. Finally, I would like to express special appreciation to the staff at Lerner Publications for its work in the production of the series.

Fred Neff

INTRODUCTION

Through the ages, people have sometimes been forced to defend themselves. Early humans probably defended themselves against animals and other human beings by using brute strength, or by hiding from their enemies or outrunning them. As time passed, however, people developed weapons such as clubs, spears, and knives with which to defend themselves.

The ancient Chinese developed a system of fighting in which the human body itself was used as a means of defense or as a weapon for attack. This system of fighting today is known as *karate*.

The Japanese developed another method of combat called *jujitsu*. This system of self-defense taught a person how to stop an attack by blocking an opponent's blows and by throwing the opponent off balance or by striking.

Although karate and jujitsu are growing in popularity among modern people, their fighting techniques are sometimes difficult. They can be done only with proper training. For example, in traditional karate, jumping kicks are one means of stopping an attacker. But the agility and precision required to do jumping kicks can be acquired only through years of practice.

Because of the special techniques taught in the traditional Asian fighting arts and the time required to learn them, a simpler method of self-defense is needed. This book was designed to fill that need.

Although the self-defense techniques presented in the following chapters are drawn from the traditional Asian fighting arts, they are relatively simple techniques that have been selected for their effectiveness and ease of use. Almost anyone can learn them. Teachers and advanced students of karate and jujitsu, as well as beginners, will find this book a helpful guide to practical self-defense.

All students are advised to read the chapters in the order in which they are presented. Students should then think about what each chapter says and follow up with practice. Practice is really the key to learning self-defense.

COMMON QUESTIONS ABOUT SELF-DEFENSE

As a beginning self-defense student, you are probably curious about what you will be learning. Although it is impossible to answer all of your questions in one chapter, there are a few common questions asked by almost all beginning students. These questions are best answered before you begin your training. Any other questions you have will probably be answered in the remaining chapters of the book.

1. How long will it take me to become an expert in self-defense?

It takes years of practice and hard work for anyone to become an expert in self-defense. A beginning student cannot become an expert simply by reading books on the subject. Students interested in becoming really skilled at self-defense should take classroom instruction from a qualified teacher as well as read books. There are no shortcuts to learning self-defense. It requires time, effort, and constant practice.

2. Can I learn self-defense techniques by watching television and movies?

Copying self-defense techniques shown in the movies and on television is not a good idea. In order to capture viewer interest, television and movie producers often use showy techniques that are exciting to watch but not practical. These techniques rarely work in real-life situations. Television shows and movies are made to entertain people rather than instruct them.

3. How can I develop enough self-confidence to stand up to an attacker?

Beginning self-defense students should realize that the fighting techniques they are practicing will work in real-life situations. Simply by familiarizing themselves with these techniques through practice, beginners will feel their self-confidence grow. Also, they must learn to have faith in their own fighting abilities. Students who believe in themselves will gain the self-confidence necessary to cope with any fighting situation.

4. Should I let others know that I have studied self-defense so that they will respect me?

No student of self-defense should brag about his or her fighting skills. A person will probably make enemies rather than gain respect by boasting. Most serious students of self-defense follow the ancient jujitsu idea that respect is earned through good deeds and kindness.

THE BASIC PRINCIPLES OF SELF-DEFENSE

Every student of self-defense should begin training by learning six basic principles, or rules. These principles act as a framework for the actual fighting techniques described in the following chapters.

1. Avoid Fights

The best way to keep from getting hurt is to avoid fights whenever possible. Staying away from trouble is no disgrace, and every self-defense student must learn the self-control necessary to keep out of a fight. Threatening or insulting words are best forgotten.

When faced by a real attacker, though, you should be aware of a variety of self-defense techniques. The only time these techniques should be used is when you are in real danger of being harmed.

2. Remain Calm

Remain calm if threatened. Staying calm helps you to think and act quickly, which may keep you from being injured. A calm mind enables you to decide more easily how to distract your attacker and which fighting techniques to use.

Another advantage of remaining calm is that you will seem very confident to an attacker. Your apparent self-confidence will give your attacker the impression that you are not afraid of him or her. Few people want to attack a person who appears willing to fight.

3. Distract Your Attacker

If you are being attacked, you should first attempt to distract your attacker. Distracting the attacker gives you time to break his or her hold or to counterattack. Distractions may make the difference between successfully defending yourself and being seriously injured.

Yelling or throwing an object are two examples of distractions that can be used. Or, if you are grabbed by the arm, you could distract your attacker with a quick hand movement before kicking him or her in the knee. The hand movement should successfully distract the attacker long enough for you to place a powerful kick.

Practice distraction techniques with a partner so that you will be in the habit of diverting your attacker's attention before you attempt a counterattack.

4. Be Aware of Your Attacker's Weak Spots

One of the secrets of self-defense is to be aware of your attacker's weak spots. Every attacker has some weak spot that can be easily exploited. For example, if an attacker lays hands on your shoulders while facing you, the attacker's face, groin, and knees are open for counterattack. If you are aware of these weak spots and quickly take action, you probably will have an advantage over your attacker.

5. Use a Combination of Fighting Techniques

Sometimes a single blow to a sensitive body area will stop an attacker. You should always plan ahead, however, so that if one technique does not end the fight, another will. For example, following a kick with a quick punch should take your attacker by surprise. A combination of techniques, such as a low kick to the knees and a high punch to the chest, makes it very difficult for the attacker to block your counter-attack.

6. Kick

Kicks are very useful in self-defense situations. The best kicks for self-defense are powerful kicks thrown low on the attacker's body. Kicks that are thrown above the attacker's waist can be blocked more easily. The person throwing a high kick can also be unbalanced more easily.

High kicks, such as those thrown to the chest and head, are best left to the self-defense experts, who have years of practice behind them. Even after years of practice, these experts are reluctant to throw high kicks. High kicks are thrown only if there is no other opening on the attacker.

EXERCISES FOR SELF-DEFENSE

Your body is better able to perform a variety of fighting techniques when its muscles are loose and flexible. By warming up with exercises, you can avoid straining muscles while practicing punches or kicks.

As a beginning self-defense student, you should avoid stretching your muscles too much at any given practice session. It is far better to stretch slowly, day by day, than to risk injuring your muscles.

WARM-UP EXERCISES
Push-Ups

Begin the exercise by lying face down on the floor. With the weight of your body resting on your knuckles and toes, raise yourself by straightening your bent arms. Then lower yourself to the ground. Rapidly repeat this process several times to increase the strength of your chest and arm muscles.

Muscle Tension Exercise

Place your right fist firmly in the palm of your left hand. For a count of three push your fist against your palm, and then relax. Repeat several times. This exercise can be done anyplace, at any time, and will increase chest and arm strength.

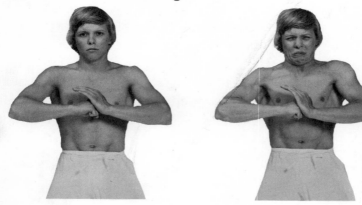

Front-Bending Exercise

From an erect stance, bend down and touch the floor with the palms of your hands. Do not bend your knees. Repeat several times. This stretching exercise will help increase the flexibility of your legs, waist, and back.

Sit-Ups

Lie on the floor, with hands at your sides. Sit up, touch your toes with your hands, and return to the lying-down position. Repeat this exercise several times. Sit-ups strengthen stomach muscles as well as increase the flexibility of the spinal column.

Body-Twisting Exercise

Stand with your feet apart and your knees slightly bent. Then, with your arms straight out from your sides, twist your body at the waist as far as you can in each direction. This exercise strengthens the back and waist muscles and increases their flexibility.

Leg-Stretching Exercise

Stand relaxed, with the feet together. Alternately kick each leg as high as it will go without bending the knee. To increase leg flexibility, kick as high as possible.

Basic Flexibility Exercise

From a relaxed stance, spread your legs apart. Spread them as far apart as possible without straining the muscles. Increase the spread with each practice session.

SPECIAL FALLING EXERCISES

Learning to fall properly is most important to good self-defense. People who know how to fall properly are less likely to suffer injury when attacked. Knowing how to fall also gives beginning students self-confidence so that they will no longer fear being thrown to the ground.

For these reasons, beginning self-defense students should practice falling. There are three things students should do when practicing: warm up with exercises so that the muscles are loose and flexible; use large mats to avoid injuries; and go through each falling exercise slowly at first to develop proper form.

Falling Back

This exercise will help the self-defense student become accustomed to falling backward when pushed or thrown by an attacker.

Assume a squatting position, with the chin tucked in and the arms extended in front of the body. Allow the body to fall backward and, at the same time, raise the extended arms. Keep the chin tucked in while falling. Just as you fall back on the mat, snap your arms down so that the forearms slap the mat about six inches (15 centimeters) from the body. This action will help absorb the impact of the fall.

Falling to the Side

Knowing how to fall to the side is helpful, should you ever be tripped or thrown by a leg sweep, a foot sweep, a shoulder throw, or a hip throw.

Assume a squatting position, with one leg crossed over the other at the ankles. Then slide the front leg forward until you lose your balance. At the same time, raise the arm of the side on which you are going to fall. Just before your body hits the mat, beat the palm of your hand against the mat to absorb the blow. This landing should keep your knees, ankles, and other sensitive areas of the body from being injured.

2.

BASIC HAND POSITIONS AND SENSITIVE AREAS OF THE HUMAN BODY

Certain parts of the human body are extremely sensitive to pain while other parts are capable of taking great punishment. For that reason, throwing a hard punch or kick to any part of the attacker's body is no guarantee that you will end a fight. You must strike a pain-sensitive area to bring the fight to an immediate end.

The two anatomy charts in this chapter point out the sensitive areas of the human body at which all strikes should be aimed. Also included in the chapter are hand positions that are taken from the Asian fighting arts. Each hand position has a particular advantage for fighting and is best used against certain parts of the human body. A good student of self-defense will always keep these hand positions in mind when choosing a striking area on the opponent's body.

BASIC HAND POSITIONS FOR HITTING

In order to avoid injury, beginning self-defense students should learn to hold their hands correctly when hitting. Before students throw actual punches and strikes, they should practice the various hand positions.

The Open Hand

Tighten the fingers of your open hand and bend their tips down slightly. Fold the end of the thumb down so that it rests against the palm. Use the outer edge of the hand to make contact with the target.

The open hand is used for attacking the head, neck, and ribs.

The Closed Fist

A proper closed fist is made by tightly folding the fingers into the palm and placing the thumb across the forefinger. The first and second knuckles of the fist should make contact with the target.

The closed fist can be used against the head, chest, and stomach.

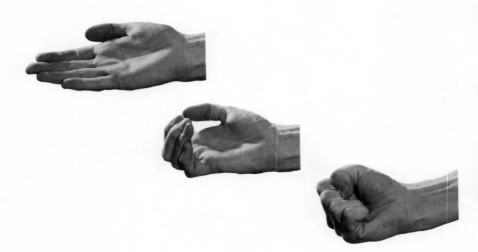

The Extended One-Knuckle Fist

The extended one-knuckle fist is formed in the same way as the closed fist, except that the middle finger is pushed forward slightly. This position makes the extended one-knuckle fist very effective against the temples and the solar plexus.

The Backfist

The backfist is made in exactly the same way as the closed fist. With the backfist, however, the knuckles and the back of the hand are used to strike.

The backfist is best used against the opponent's face, chest, and ribs.

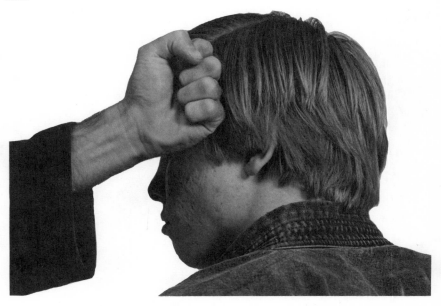

SENSITIVE AREAS OF THE HUMAN BODY

To be effective fighters, beginning students should learn early in their training the body areas sensitive to pain. All striking techniques should be directed toward these pain-sensitive areas.

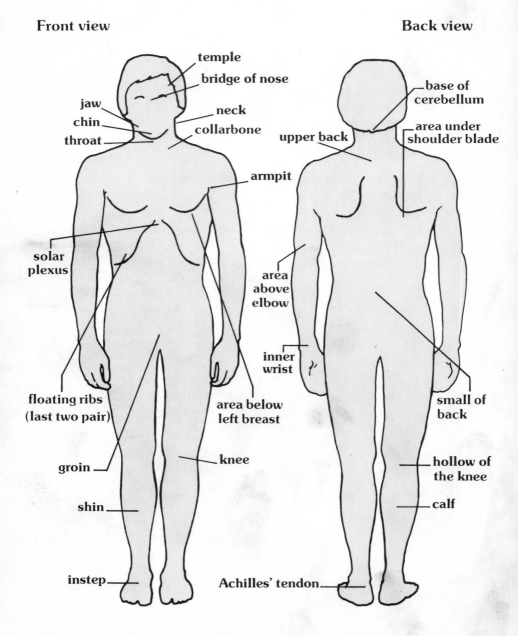

Front view

- temple
- bridge of nose
- jaw
- chin
- neck
- throat
- collarbone
- armpit
- solar plexus
- floating ribs (last two pair)
- area below left breast
- groin
- knee
- shin
- instep
- Achilles' tendon

Back view

- base of cerebellum
- area under shoulder blade
- upper back
- area above elbow
- inner wrist
- small of back
- hollow of the knee
- calf

3.
SELF-DEFENSE STANCES

A strong stance is very important to good self-defense. When a person is standing in a stable position, an attacker will have great difficulty in throwing him or her to the ground. Another reason a strong stance is important is that it allows a person to throw a punch or a kick without risking loss of balance. Also, an attacker will probably be reluctant to fight anyone who assumes a strong fighting stance when threatened.

The beginning self-defense student should practice changing from one stance to another with smooth, graceful motions. This will enable the student to shift body positions quickly and easily in a real-life situation.

The Horse Stance

The horse stance is a flexible stance that can be used for blocking, kicking, or punching.

To assume this stance, stand with your feet parallel and about two shoulder-widths apart. Your torso should be erect and its weight evenly distributed between your legs. Your knees should be bent as if you were riding a horse. Your hands should be made into closed fists, held palms up and positioned slightly above the hips.

The Modified Horse Stance

The modified horse stance is the best all-around stance for self-defense. Because the body is well balanced, blocks, kicks, punches, and throws can easily be started from this position.

To assume the stance, place one leg directly in front of the other leg, two shoulder-widths apart. Bend the knees and carry your weight evenly on both legs. Keep the torso erect. Keep your forward hand open and held in front of you at about waist level. Make the other hand into a fist and hold it slightly above the rear hip.

The Back Stance

In the back stance, a large part of the body weight is carried on the rear leg. Because of the strong rear support, the back stance gives stability for blocking. It is also a good stance from which to throw front kicks.

To assume the back stance, place one leg in front of the other so that the feet are approximately one-and-one-half shoulder-widths apart. The rear leg should be deeply bent and carry about 70 percent of the body's weight. The forward leg should be slightly bent and carry the remainder of the body's weight.

The forward hand should be open and held in front of the body at about waist level. The other hand, in fist position, should be held slightly above the rear hip, palm upward.

4.
DODGING OR BLOCKING PUNCHES AND KICKS

Perhaps the most important part of self-defense is learning to dodge or block an attacker's punches and kicks. No matter how skilled a self-defense student becomes at throwing punches and kicks, he or she will not have time to counterattack without dodging or blocking. This chapter will show how to dodge and block an attack; later chapters on hand and foot techniques will deal with counterattack.

To better simulate a real attack, practice dodging and blocking with a partner. All blocks should be practiced slowly at first, and the pace should be increased only as the student gains self-confidence.

DODGES
Leaning to the Side

A defender should dodge to one side or another when a punch or a kick is thrown toward the neck or head. Dodging to the side of a punch is a good tactic if the defender is not in a fighting stance but is standing with his or her feet parallel.

To successfully dodge a punch or a kick, bend at the waist to one side. At the same time, shift most of your body weight to the leg on the side to which you are bending.

Leaning to the Rear

Leaning back quickly is a good way to dodge a punch directed toward the head. The modified horse stance is the best stance for this dodge.

As the attacker throws the punch toward your head, bend backward at the waist and shift most of your weight to the rear leg. Move quickly so that the attacker's punch falls short of its target.

Stepping to the Rear

If you are standing relaxed, feet together and hands at your sides, and see a punch coming toward your head, quickly step to the rear so that you are in a modified horse stance. At the same time, bend backward at the waist so that the attacker's punch falls short of your face.

BLOCKS
The Upper-Level Block

The upper-level block is used to deflect punches directed toward the chest and head. This block can be carried out from any fighting stance.

When an attacker releases a punch, raise your blocking arm to meet the blow. Your blocking arm should deflect the blow up and away from you. In blocking an attack, the outside of your forearm should come in contact with the inside of the attacker's extended punching arm.

If possible, look your attacker in the eyes before he or she throws a punch. The movements of the eyes often give away the attacker's intended target. For example, if an attacker intends to throw a punch at your chest, he or she will probably look in that direction before releasing the punch.

Blocking with the Palm of the Hand

The palms of the hands can be used to deflect an attacker's punch. Blocking with the palms can be done from any fighting stance and will best deflect blows directed toward the head and the mid-body.

Of the two kinds of palm blocks, the single- and the double-palm, the double-palm is the easiest. To do the double-palm block, simply bring the palms of your hands up to meet the outer part of the attacker's punching arm. One of your palms should be braced against the attacker's wrist while the other is held against the upper arm. When your hands make contact with the attacker's arm, push it away.

double-palm block

single-palm block

The single-palm block, though similar to the double-palm block, is more difficult to execute. Because the success of this block depends on the speed and accuracy of a single hand, a beginning self-defense student is better off learning the double-palm block first. By practicing the double-palm block, the student will develop the coordination and speed necessary to block with a single hand.

In the single-palm block, you will use only one hand to block the attacker's punch. With the fingers of the blocking hand squeezed tightly together, push against the wrist of the attacker's arm.

The Mid-Level Block

The mid-level block is used for deflecting blows directed toward the chest and stomach. This block can be carried out from any fighting stance.

When a punch is thrown toward your chest or stomach, bring your arm up with a snapping motion. The hard inside edge of your forearm should deflect your attacker's arm. Make sure that your elbow is firmly bent.

The Lower-Level Block

The lower-level block, or downward block, is used to deflect blows intended for the stomach and groin. This block can be done from any fighting stance.

To execute the block, bring the blocking arm up across the body as you drop the hand of the other arm in front of the groin. (By placing your hand in front of the groin, you are giving added protection in the event that your block is less than successful.) The blocking arm should then be brought out and down to deflect the attacker's punch or kick. A successful block should direct the force of the attack away from the body. After the blow is deflected, the hand protecting the groin should be held just above the hip, a position that readies the hand for counterattack.

The Low Cross-Block

The low cross-block is very effective in stopping strong front kicks directed toward the lower part of the body. This block, which makes use of crossed arms, can be done from any fighting stance.

To fend off a kick, make fists, cross your arms, and push your crossed arms downward to meet the blow. The attacker's kick will be caught between your fists. It is most important not to lean too far forward while blocking—you could lose your balance.

5.

COUNTERATTACKING WITH PUNCHES AND STRIKES

The hands, if properly trained, are marvelous weapons for self-defense and counterattack. Throughout Asia, the hands have long been considered strong weapons of self-defense. The ancient Chinese developed several systems of self-defense based on striking and thrusting techniques of the hand. The Japanese also developed various striking techniques that made use of the hands and arms. These ancient Oriental techniques included fist attacks, open-hand strikes, forearm strikes, and elbow strikes.

This chapter is designed to show practical hand techniques selected from the various Asian fighting arts. The beginning self-defense student should practice each technique until it becomes almost automatic.

The Open-Hand Blow

The open-hand blow, one of the most versatile of all striking techniques, can be used to attack an opponent's head, neck, or ribs. It can be executed from any stance.

There are many self-defense situations in which you can use an open-hand blow. One of the most common situations is to strike at the opponent just as he or she is about to attack. As the opponent moves forward, bring your striking arm up across your body. Your elbow should be bent and your hand properly positioned for an open-hand blow. Twist your body toward the opponent as your striking arm snaps toward the target. Your arm should be straight when the striking hand makes contact with the target. Contact with the target should be made only with the outer edge of the hand.

The open-hand blow can also be used when an attacker reaches out to grab you. As the attacker reaches for you, strike hard with an open-hand blow to the attacker's forearm. Try to hit a sensitive area, or pain center, hard enough to discourage the opponent from fighting.

The open-hand blow is also a good follow-up to a block. When your opponent throws a punch, deflect it with a palm block and then strike down on the opponent's neck with an open-hand blow.

The Forefist Punch

The forefist punch, a strong counterattack technique, is the most commonly used punching method. The punch begins with the fist at the side of the body, palm upward. As the punch is thrown directly forward, the fist twists so that the palm is turned down when the arm is fully extended. The twisting action puts more power in the punch.

The forefist punch, delivered to the head or chest, is best used after blocking an attack. One forefist punch should immediately be followed by another so that the attacker is stopped and the fight brought quickly to an end.

The Backfist Blow

The backfist blow is a powerful technique that can be used to attack an opponent's head, chest, or ribs. To execute the backfist blow, bring your forearm upward with a snapping motion of the elbow so that the back of your fist strikes the target.

The Backfist Blow (continued)

Use the backfist blow as your attacker moves toward you or when you are grabbed from the front or the rear.

To escape from an attacker who is attempting to pin one arm behind you, twist your body toward him or her and strike hard with a backfist. The back of the hand should strike with such force that the attacker releases you.

The Extended One-Knuckle Blow

The extended one-knuckle blow is a very effective technique when used against an attacker's solar plexus or any other sensitive area of the body.

If an attacker rests both hands on your shoulders to keep you from moving, simply punch upward to the solar plexus with your fist palm up. The middle finger of your fist should be slightly extended so that its knuckle can strike deeply into the attacker's sensitive area.

Hitting with the extended one-knuckle blow also will force an attacker to release a hold or a lock. To break a powerful grip, strike down hard on the back of your opponent's hand with an extended one-knuckle blow. If your opponent does not immediately release you, do not give up. Keep hitting until your attacker loosens his or her grip. Because the back of the hand is sensitive and cannot stand repeated blows, your attacker should soon release you.

The Elbow Strike

The elbow strike is an extremely useful fighting technique, because most attackers do not expect elbows to be used against them. The element of surprise and the fact that the elbow strike can be executed from any stance make it an excellent technique for self-defense.

If you are grabbed from behind, forcefully swing your hip and elbow backward. Your elbow should make contact with the attacker's face, chest, or stomach.

6.

COUNTERATTACKING WITH THE FEET

The graceful kicks of karate and kung fu have excited people in the western world as no other Asian fighting techniques have. Self-defense students should realize, however, that kicking is not as easy as it seems in the movies. Each kicking technique must be practiced many times before it becomes a practical weapon for self-defense.

Kicking, like other fighting techniques, has both advantages and disadvantages. One disadvantage of kicking is that a kick is sometimes easy to spot and block. Also, if a kick is executed slowly or at too high a level, an attacker can more easily throw the kicker off balance. The two main advantages of kicking are power and range: the human leg, because of its great strength, is able to deliver a powerful blow; and a kick, because of the leg's length, has considerable range.

Because of the advantages and disadvantages to both hand and foot fighting, a good self-defense student will try to use a combination of techniques. Hand and foot fighting used together are most effective. If only one technique is used, however, the defending person risks a weakness in defense that can be exploited by the attacker.

The following foot-fighting techniques should be practiced along with related hand techniques. By practicing certain foot- and hand-fighting techniques together, the self-defense student will be better equipped for an encounter with a real attacker.

The Front Kick

The powerful front kick is best used against an attacker's knees, groin, stomach, chest, or head. It is an especially useful method of stopping an opponent who is moving forward to attack.

To execute a good front kick, bend the knee of the kicking leg and lift it up toward your chest just as your attacker approaches. Then straighten the raised leg so that the ball of the foot hits the attacker with great force. It is usually a good idea to follow up a low kick with a forefist punch to the attacker's head. .

The front kick can also be used for counterattack after the attacker's punch has been blocked. To follow a block, use a combination of hand and foot techniques, such as a front kick to the attacker's shin with a one-knuckle punch to the solar plexus.

The Side Kick

If you are attacked from the side, bend the knee of your kicking leg and pull the knee up toward your chest. Then thrust your leg out from the side of your body so that your heel hits the attacker.

49

The Back Kick

When you believe that you will be attacked from the rear, turn your head so that you can see behind you. Bend the knee of your kicking leg and thrust the kicking leg directly to the rear, using the snap of the knee to firmly plant the bottom of your foot on the target.

The Stamping Kick

The stamping kick is used for striking an opponent's knees, shins, or feet. When your opponent grabs you from the front, raise the bent knee of your kicking leg and thrust that leg out and down so that your heel strikes the opponent's knee, shin, or foot. The stamping kick is an excellent means of distracting your opponent's attention long enough for you to throw a middle- or high-level punch without being blocked.

The Ground Kick

The ground kick enables a person who has been thrown to the ground to fight off an attacker. A properly executed ground kick usually catches the attacker off guard. Most attackers do not expect their victims to continue fighting once they have been thrown to the ground.

When an attacker pushes you down with your back to the ground, immediately bring both knees up to your chest. At the same time, position your body so that your feet are aimed at the attacker. As the attacker moves toward you, thrust one leg and then the other toward the attacker's groin, knees, or shins. Do not attempt to get off the ground until the attacker has retreated from your counterattack. Ready your hands for punching, in the event that your foot defense is less than successful.

7.
THROWS AND ESCAPES

Most students learn early in their training that there is more to self-defense than knowing how to execute a few blocks, punches, and kicks. They learn that it is sometimes necessary to throw an opponent or to slip out of a painful hold.

To successfully execute throws and escape tactics in real fights, self-defense students must remember to remain calm, use distractions, take advantage of the element of surprise, and know their self-defense techniques so well that they can be done automatically.

Beginning students, especially, should practice self-defense techniques with partners so that they can accustom themselves to properly using throws and escape tactics in real-life situations. During practice sessions: 1. Mats must always be used, and safety must never be forgotten; 2. Partners who have not learned the falling exercises should not be thrown; 3. Practice throws should be executed gently as a safeguard against injuries; 4. Practice partners should never be thrown at full force.

Keep in mind that all self-defense movements, especially throws, should be practiced slowly and gently at first. Only when both practice partners agree that they feel comfortable using certain techniques should the training get harder and the pace of execution speed up.

Finally, self-defense students should agree, before practicing, to tap one another on the arm or to say "enough" if a hold or fighting technique is done with too much force. Upon feeling a tap or hearing "enough," a student should release his or her partner.

THROWS
The Outside Sweeping-Leg Throw

The outside sweeping-leg throw can be used in many different self-defense situations. When an attacker throws a punch at you, deflect the blow with a palm block. Then get a firm grip on your attacker's arm and shoulder and push him or her backward. At the same time, slip your right leg behind your opponent's right leg. To throw the opponent, continue to push him or her backward, and sweep your right leg behind you.

The Inside Sweeping-Leg Throw

The inside sweeping-leg throw is extremely effective against an attacker whose legs are wide apart. When your opponent has a tight grip on you, turn your right hip toward the opponent and insert your right leg between his or her legs. Push the opponent backward with your hands as you sweep the opponent's left leg out from under him or her with the back of your right leg.

The Shoulder Throw

The shoulder throw is a powerful throw that can be used to end a fight quickly. When an attacker throws a high punch, block it with your left arm and immediately place your right foot in front of the attacker's right foot. Then, using your right foot as a pivot, swing your body around so that your back is against the attacker's front. As you pivot, bring your right arm under the attacker's right armpit and reach around to grab him or her by the shoulder. You should also grip the attacker's arm with your left hand as you pull him or her forward and onto your back, ready to be thrown. Your knees should be bent at this time. To complete the throw, straighten your legs and force your hips up and back as you pull the attacker over your right shoulder.

The shoulder throw is an extremely effective technique for a short person to use on a taller person. The short person has the advantage of easily fitting his or her shoulder under the taller person's armpit.

ESCAPES
Escaping from a Wrist Grip

When an attacker grabs your wrist, reach across your body with your free hand and firmly grip your other hand. Break the hold by pulling with both hands. This motion will free the imprisoned wrist by forcing it between the attacker's thumb and forefinger, thus breaking the grip.

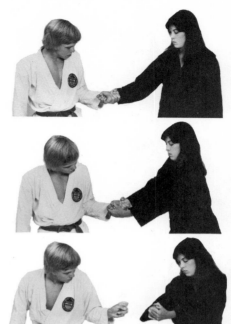

This escape technique also works when an attacker has a grip on both of your wrists. To escape, simply use one jerky motion to pull your wrists out through the weak spot in the attacker's grip.

In many fighting situations, it is advisable to begin your escape with a low kick to your attacker's shins, a distracting technique that will enable you to pull out of his or her grip more easily.

Escaping from a Forearm Choke

When an attacker uses his or her forearm to choke you from behind, you can relieve the pressure by pulling down hard on the arm around your neck. At the same time, kick back into the attacker's knee or shin. Follow up with an elbow strike to the ribs or stomach and a stamp on the instep of the attacker's foot. When the choke hold is loosened, slip your body downward and to the rear. Quickly bring the attacker's choking arm up behind his or her back and apply pressure.

Escaping from a Rear Double-Hand Choke

When an attacker uses his or her hands to choke you from behind, simply grab the smallest finger on each of the attacker's hands and pull sharply outward. Then kick backward into the attacker's shins and lift the choking hands off your neck.

Escaping from a Headlock

If your opponent has your head encircled with his or her arms, you are trapped in a headlock. To break the headlock, slip your leg behind the attacker's nearest leg and deeply bend your knees. At the same time, sweep your arm back and over the attacker's nearest shoulder and place your cupped hand firmly on the attacker's chin. Push the chin backward as you lift the attacker's leg off the ground with your free hand. In the final step, throw the attacker to the ground.

Another method of escaping from a headlock is to kick down on the back of the attacker's knee and, at the same time, grab his or her hair and yank it backward.

Back view

Escaping from a Rear Waist Hold

If you are grabbed around the waist from behind, quickly spread your legs and bend forward. Follow up with several one-knuckle blows to the back of the attacker's hand to loosen his or her grip. Then quickly reach down between your legs, grab your attacker's ankle and pull it upward, thus forcing him or her to fall backward.

INDEX

ABOUT THE AUTHOR

Fred Neff has been a student of the Asian fighting arts for most of his life. He started his training at the age of eight and eventually specialized in karate. Today Mr. Neff holds the rank of fifth degree black belt in that fighting art. In addition to karate, he is also proficient in judo and jujitsu. For many years, Mr. Neff has used his knowledge of the Asian fighting arts to educate others. He has taught karate at the University of Minnesota, the University of Wisconsin, and Hamline University and Inver Hills College in St. Paul, Minnesota. He has also organized and supervised self-defense classes in public schools, private schools, and in city recreation departments. Included in his teaching program have been classes for law enforcement officers.

Fred Neff graduated with high distinction from the University of Minnesota College of Education in 1970. In 1976, he received his J.D. degree from William Mitchell College of Law in St. Paul, Minnesota. Mr. Neff is now a practicing attorney in Minneapolis, Minnesota.